EAT THE DAMN PIE

Linda Spolidoro

YesNo Press

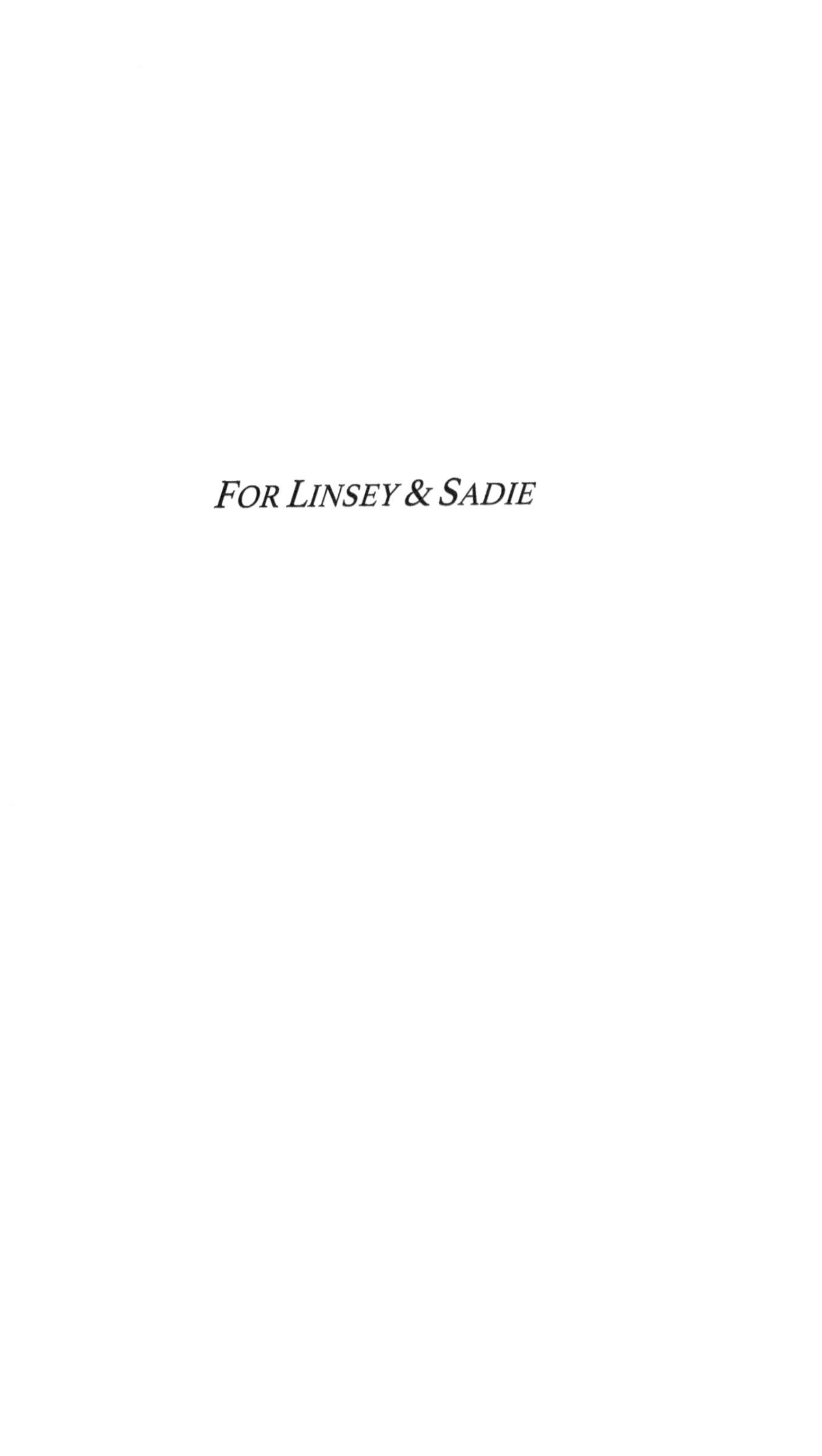

FOR LINSEY & SADIE

Table of Contents

between us, I've grown sharp edges—
sliding into sideburns like lips

that don't belong to that face, oil slicked
or petroleum jelly, or baking soda to ward off

infection. Have you heard anything I've said?
Have we met where you are? I've been there—

ate second-rate oreo cookies there—top first, then
mouse finger the edges, a little cream filled

oasis for the patient—I'm not patient, I just like looking
forward to something. If you attacked me, blood

lust and murder in your muggers' eyes, I would
accept it, recall the neighbor girl, dirty and alone—

the trick we played, my sister, my brother, and I
told her, bullied her to eat that rotten apple off the ground

evil step-mothered her, then consoled her as she cried
her blue-eyes, or gray, or maybe brown like the rot

there is poison in the ground, plastic in breast milk—
my mother said my skin was too thin and I'd better

thank my lucky stars or *Jesus, Mary, and Joseph*
she'd give me something to cry about—

her song following me away, all fifteen
ripe for the picking, twisted up years of me

"Oh Momma you're so big and fat
it must be jelly cuz jam don't shake like that"

mothers, have you heard me?
I've been where you are—still motherless

there is poison leached into the earth, in her milk—
of course my skin is thin

confession

you do not sit
but kneel subservient
as the tiny slant door
is fingered open
you speak to an ear, a cheek
a side-eyed middle-man
he never looks directly at you
not to spare you any discomfort
but to reinforce the power
of peripheral vision

he knows guilt only hurts from the inside out
while humiliation can be carried
like a sick and panting dog across
the shoulders
it's a glass eye
or a deformed appendage
a rip up the back of your pants

you know by now
the redundancy of children blushing
the waste of rushed blood
I mean, you can never go back far enough
you are born blighted
your babydoll body scrubbed
sinless with holy water and prayer
doused in smoky recitations
and later, when you could perhaps
put this whole ugly thing behind you
you are marked each year with ashes
an annual and ancient thumbprint pushed
into the center of your forehead
so you'll never forget

Jack Ruby

This isn't about Jack Ruby / or the cheering yourself with childbirth / or bags full of dryer lint / or the little brother of your little brother / or his fat stupid fingers / his obvious mediocrity / the answer to every question he's ever asked / always the name of his first pet / always the boy / always his stupid penis / folding arms over chest / and you at the top of the stairs.

Remember that time you shat tar for a week and woke up not in your bed but in a room where a girl with vintage Mia Farrow shorn hair and a bamboo robe sobbed the names of people you did not know, and the people you did know were someplace else pearling another oyster with better prospects?

This is not about Valerie Solanas / or the murderer of the murderer / or the failed assassin of the failed marriage / or the abortion you had when you were in love and beaten bloody.

This is not about suffering / or the carving of sins into the underbelly of the straight back chair / its metal feet scraping linoleum / *remember how well your blue woolen blazer bore the hook?* / never meeting god.

This is about your baby, pushing its way out, its blue body covered in milk, a rosy hued stamp, birth-marked above its right eye, a proclamation: *Now, you are this.* But the mother of the mother (she is never the blanket) peels back muscle till a cage of bone cowers: *No, little girl, you are this.*

the last low end
where my grandfather worked
where at sixteen my uncle lost the tip
of his finger
a flood of rain spilled fumes up through
the rust-hole floor of the blue nova

surrounded by ancestral ghosts
that could not protect me
could not unhaunt
the glove of bruises at my wrists
could not return the red river
reverse the tender prey
of bad mothering
or re-wild the wanderer

instead engined a whir
a warning
the drone-like hum of a hundred
sorrowful wives dirging in waves
a fist at the granite tombs

& the boy next door
smells of gas and exhaust
cuts my lawn while I'm out
& then *he* thanks me
he wants to sleep with me
but does not know
that I am the clover
& the bee
& the honey
& there is simply no place left
that has not been stung
or plucked
or crushed
or crowded out
& so I tinfoil a baked offering

sit bare-legged inside his savor
breathe in the fumes
& wait for the grass to grow

14

if you backward me a flight pattern
hit repeat, repeat, repeat
would the spring peepers
pissing into the palm of my hand

venture back to the surface—
hollow upward into the green
litter of pitted deformities
that is the past tense of apples

at my first concert—
Jethro Tull played a flute
dragged a burlap sack onto the stage
while he cross-eyed a Mary song

and I got arrested in a parking lot
behind a building on the way home
because boys like to hold it in the palm
of their hands—piss everywhere

not unlike the communal squatting
of my female ancestors
without shame or hesitation—
filling hollows and tending wounds—

at the end of the show, and only
after the encore, a disheveled girl—
released by a man in a tunic
rushed off stage—
after 2 hours in a sack—
(presumably)
to take a piss

who did not like me

I was hard to please
my mother said
wore the wrong width
the wrong grin
pushed too hard
on the way out
& so I tangled
the phone wires
frayed them
pulled them from the base
blamed the cat

I killed the neighbor boy
he stabbed me in the chest
with a broken piece
of his father's pontiac
& from there on out
I hated myself
loved my mother more
but only on the inside
where no one could see
& it didn't count

I didn't really kill the boy
I thought about it
I mean they might have believed
the cat was a wire-tangling vandal
but a murderer?

so instead I wore my arms
like an X
like an old-timey corpse
kept a bowl of pennies
by my bed

woke up cold on the inside
decided not to give up

my old landline
with its wires
& its faux rotary design
—it doesn't ring anymore
& I haven't answered
that ghost in years
but you see
I've always had a talent
for complicating
the simplest things

it's true

i should have listened to my mother
when she called me a trollop
she would eventually be right
& my downfall arrived shaggy
in a leather vest dragging a crooked leg

i'd have bit the tip off that mirage
& filled my pockets with rocks
if i hadn't forced the heart to heal

less an erasure than a dream
of mutual suicide
or a good spaghetti dinner
on a soggy paper plate

it's like it always is
when one wishes
to be somewhere else
immovable
the road branches of february
brittle, joyless
a starch still grimace

i assure you there is no comfort
hearing the snap & crack
of the body-weak, un-bearing branches
less a nailing tree than a ghost story

& i knew who would be the end boss
the hand-chopper of the graffiti artist
the brow-beater of angry erection
the volcano's forced tribute

there is no magic here
just the self-immolation of acceptance
more a bloody gash than a boast
& i ask only out of a sense of decorum

if you must invisible me
send me to my knees at thirteen
at least break out the good china

she kneels
head tilted
eyes closed in mock prayer
her legs tingle with the quick
pricked sensation of spider bites
her heart so full that it spills
into her belly where the spiders
have laid eggs, hatching
and filling her with poison
rising into her throat
passing rapturously
into her fevered brain—
like the veil of a bride or a widow

she tugs the navy-blue socks
above the sharp contour
of her boney catholic knees
kneels on marble
stairs reserved
for holy men
—only men
while the specter of christ
dead or dying
in the throes of a last ecstasy
rains down
the truth about us all
in sickness, sickness

The Imp of the Perverse

There is a woman in Kentucky who makes little coffins for women who have miscarriages. Her husband would like to give them names and birth certificates too.

Had I known this 17 years ago, I might have buried upwards of 8 tiny coffins,
run out of all the good baby names, and spent more time veiled and in black

than is necessary for the normal, everyday, interaction avoidance I've perfected.
I once cut clear through my hand with a bread knife. Holding the roll lengthwise

in the palm of my hand, my father's voice ringing in my ears. "Put it on the
counter and place your hand, fingers lifted, on the top, not too much pressure,

and watch the knife, always watch the knife." I remembered this deli counter
wisdom as I wrapped my hand in a towel, slid metallic cool down the door

of the refrigerator and thought about all the times I had peeled and chopped
vegetables for stew, or soup, or company, imagining my fingers were carrots.

I'm sure there is a name for this urge to cut off one's own fingers.
But I don't know it. So instead, I'll make each severed finger a tiny coffin.

by accident

we drank rum and the cans of coke—fluttering rose little bubbles
that popped cracking whole icebergs apart like a Norse god

with a hammer—your head resting on the slow savage movements
of a million red ants, filling the space between the hollow

mattress and the broken rib the doctor said would heal on its own—
you winced shock when the bellyflop went so hysterically wrong

and the breath left your body momentarily sucked into the galaxy
of a pinprick helium balloon—we still had atmosphere the night

we danced sweaty at the bar next to the House of Corrections
and I visited you once in jail before you took my name off the list

so I couldn't come back—we pretended to be alone in a swanky
hotel somewhere, but really more suited to motels with their decades

of semen and smoke and concrete thresholds—the men with functional
beards and pickup trucks dusted with hard thirsty work—remember

you pissed my bed drunk once? It was an accident, funny—like
both my legs in casts a week before my sister's wedding—

I remembered how you said you hated the way I used words and told me
you were hurt—I had to step behind the far corner of the house

so you wouldn't see me laughing, belly-laughing—I mean
there is nothing so funny as an accident

I hate to be the one to tell you but jesus isn't coming back for you

that threat that tired that forward empty onward
fist-hard & barked already shooting
roots long before you were born
you've not even fully branched

ah! but what a tree
to drop that silken caterpillar
onto your shoulder
the summer the driveway was
thick with them
& the sidewalks
& the gutty yellow
of the freshly mowed lawn

you got used to death that way
used to the idea that some things
die once even if
over & over again

do you think of your one death?
you should make it a mountain?
or a craven valley?
or a fish eye?
invite the oceans to wear
black & swallow tuna
sandwiches full of crusts
tooth-picked
& soggy with salt water?

you are not so special
as to be revived
pulled from a gaping hole
by the unconsolable
you may never drop like
fleshy seeds from the sky
be brushed away

with a panicked swipe
be remembered
but even you
deserve
a season

I have genuflected through a washed-up canon
cursing each bent knee
a promise of martyrdom
if only I held between my hands
a ball of smoke
so thick it made my heart black
my eyes red
drawn upward
toward the grotesque
figure of the catholics' favorite pin-up
I had a pretty cool cat once
why not roll his stone?

I mean, I enjoy a little satire as much as the next heretic
but I won't lead that lamb to the slaughterhouse
on the off chance he'll get another go
I'm no foil
I don't trust that held out hand
one finger shy of restitution
one eye blind hiding
easter eggs up his ass
where a remarkable slight of hand
baskets the whole tired affair

so send me a sign that blows a tree down
sucks a sea dry
or at the very least allows my GPS
enough wisdom to reroute

before I raised eyebrows I raised eyes
before I bent I bowed
before I spat I held a finger to the wind
and before that
I placed a tiny tomb
beneath a birch

M on the rocks

The girl, we'll call her M,
frightened the land fallow with her promise
had no more milk, entreated blood to flow in its stead

M was not unaware
knew she would lie underground for 15 million years
(give or take)

and in the end
which one would love her
would be forgiven his murderous tendencies

M was left twice by the rock
to lick salt and spin goldenrod
from something useful into paper
or a cup which holds pennies

but instead M wished
a crag of knuckled branches
like her grandmother's ringed
and useless left hand

—that pocked and inconvenient utensil
could not hold even one of the seven seas

M's god forgave her
wanted to arrest her
but could find no good reason
so he picked her bones clean
left her by the sea
to become salt

Ralph Steadman

I thought it was you who lobbed that bomb of tear gas into my window,
but it was not a bomb at all, only smoke and tears, a byproduct

of bad luck and by all accounts, a lack of gratitude. I want to say fuck
gratitude but when I fragment the sounds they form something else more

palatable considering my current occupation and the steady stream
of bows. Lately my dreams are written in Ralph Steadman letters,

they roll the windows up, push the backs of my eyeballs toward
the impasse, pin my arm behind my back and cry me to scream 'uncle'.

I'd squared a surrender one leg up before realizing it wasn't a bomb.
If only you'd ask me to get out and look up, watch the dead stars

explode into the omnipresent theater, I might crush my boundaries sit cross-
legged atop my dream of dying & resume burning June's three wishes.

I want to say patience and grace and gratitude, but what slips out is
bomb and smoke and tears.

no burnt amber whiskey dream
scrapes your brow furrow deeper than the unsevered & the unsaid
you did not wound the clock, were always a second-hand-loss
a slow backward cumulative tock
you stood sad-eyed
at the sink
called it
named it
felt it pull you
unmovable in concrete

your stupid feet not knowing any better
think that they are the attached

you didn't rug burn that flesh voluntarily—
but you don't dance with a mirror
tell it what it wants to hear & get driven
home in the morning by a three-fingered sacred
heart tattoo not to believe
in grace
& gods
& monsters

you are a deep well
you are nose & feet & all heart
but only plastic valentine memes magnetized
to tell the world the things
she does not care about
says she does
but does not even have the good sense
to kill the saboteurs
& so we must kill ourselves & we do
by the thousands
but it is not enough to satisfy grace
painted in black & white but larger lately & with more
shadow than spark
the eyes believing in math—

only math
but math does not bother
itself with anger or worry or grace
but its humor is dry

& you might miss it if you worry too much
do not think about your death
it's just more math

& the stupid you who does not know any better
still thinks that you are the attached

come tapping like tongue to palate
all steeled-toe statement queries
a c-clamp of letters and thought-bubbled
chest compressions

some men they shift like winds
forget
their mothers were girls
their Y was X
their home was me

some men they forgive easily
—themselves
transgressions
thumb their fist
shake a rattle
snake the other way 'round

some men they seethe
to the tooth
her blood
her flip
her bone
her holey
holy femme
goddess girl-friday
birth

some men they bleed
like screen doors torn
barbed
wired
where in the summer
the fruit flies live and die
in quick succession

and once to save the wine

I placed a bowl of vinegar
on the counter
and drowned them

why are you sitting in that chair opened palms to your forehead /
     don't you know there are locomotives on your shoes / you
     hobbled the track all by yourself / pulled it up tie by tie

then sat back flipping pennies into the air / a field of wildflowers
     springs up around you / but you full as a bloated tick / spit the
     weakest equivocations / from between your teeth

I have no more time to waste on your wooden wheels / spin
     something already & make it quick / that ten dollars ten years
     old tucked into my shoe unblessed / & unspent will travel

farther than I could ever breathe you awake / the daisies and the
     black-eyed susans will not even remember your name / don't
     you know the prayer coined between your fingertips / greened
     by men that whistle with their fingers

& trade in degradations like baseball cards / the wind will blow
     your sawdust body into the sea / & saturday will still throw its
     dirty socks to the floor / & leave its cups unwashed

no angel will whisper you back to life

we sat in the drudge and concrete
& I asked him how he held his name
so tightly between his teeth
how he forgot me
& how he proxied the response
I had heard so many times
it fell away

& did he know the patched lacquer
on which we stood
was the hard back of a turtle?

I didn't wait for the answer
had already turned white-eyed
pontypooled his face
his name
the way he bit down on it
that one long hair
above his right eye

& I heard him silent
say he stood nowhere
& it was nothing all the way down

before the kitchen floor
became an ocean
before the television
became two & they found their own
separate bureaus to sit on
there was that paper-thin moment

where clouds looked like horses
dancing umbrellas & lies flickered
like iridescence, like full bellies
like magic tricks when you still
liked magic
& clouds
& lies

sometimes words are fat steak dinners
painted rooms full of fragrant blooms
but eventually you rumble hungry
an alphabet of strung together
poverty of bridges drawn
gaping quiet like loneliness
but not the eyelash fluttering
toe-dip kind

the kind of loneliness that only
everyone, everywhere feels
& in response conjures a breech
birth of denial
a ceiling full
of plastic galaxies
a deep pull of appetency
to unblacken
the redacted

I'm left
in this house to remember
how we tried

to contract the uncontractable
remember loneliness
remember the ocean
was the first
thin
lie

I bend at the elbow
but only like plastic and screws
and never let my lovers go—
wrap them 'round my feet
like scraps of muslin
misery willful darts
that fall too short
become tired
and turn around—

unbent, I kneel
on marble steps
like St. Seraphim
but not marble, bees
and not kneel, but feed
and in October
the abortion dream
drops leaves from
the window tree
and I un-pray
when the un-sky
picks me down into
your porn and pillory

I am not un-laughing
the reckless pang of
the interventionist
deity—grown weary
he drops the act, doffs his hat
click, clicks heels or hooves
hangs the baby over
the bridge by
its ankles and
threatens
a flood

so you like the second layered cold snap
of death and decay, the falling detritus masked
in pretty colors that fool the willfully and easily placated
with bowls of steel-cut oatmeal *(—or gruel)* and clowns
your once utilitarian morning coffee

tis the season your neighbor embarrasses his dog
into a spider costume parading his little sad eyes around the block
while the year-round skull sits atop a dusty dictionary
noticed now and all of a sudden festive

save the possibility that the netherworld might well rise
and wave the bony fingered judgement I would fatten up
honey-heavy and hibernate bear-like till the thaw
but every year I endure the chill that brittles my darkest room

disappoint an obligation of pretend mirth and merriment
find a god or goddess
to rend the webbed fascia that prisons like winter
my once clear-eyed father

lost in forever october
the butter knife clawed and stiffening
above his morning toast
he'll remember another fall
like a hammer missing a nail

I asked if Jesus wanted to come
for dinner but he was busy
feeding the multitudes fermenting
a boatload of wine for the lepers
healing them with a wave
of his left hand & inducing the blind
to see with his right
it's a thing he likes to do in his free time
like fishing but without a net
or a pole of course
a kind of Jedi mind thing inherited
from his father & I asked him
how he did it & he said he wasn't
really sure that ever since
he was little he could do almost
anything if he put his mind to it
& that people seemed to like it
so he added some jazzier
things like walking on water or dying
& showing up three days later
looking all rested & unbloody
& I asked so this feeding the hungry
& healing the sick thing is something
that you could do all of the time
I mean like you could feed every
single person in the world
cure every sickness that ever
existed anytime you wanted?
& he said well of course but
I really think you're missing the point

The Inheritor

He confessed that he had never loved beautiful women
and that he valued imperfection in such large order
that he'd lost the ability to differentiate between
the profane and the divine—they had merged
into a lovely fusion of well-worn hardships, furrowed brows,
and barely detectable sparks of light behind the eyes

She would become his devotion, and when she
said she was full he'd convince her to eat
and when she pulled all the daisies up from their roots
he put painted rocks in their place—
and when she felt tired and ready to die
he'd wrap her body 'round his waist like rope
place her feet atop his and dance

She would eventually slip away and he'd be left
with ashes in a coffee can with the torn label still attached
and his heart too, would stop beating its doddering thump—
and all the beauty that never existed would be reduced to a prayer
he'd recite at bedtime as he climbed into her body like a coffin
pulling on top of his own, her beautiful ugly bones

About the Author

Linda Spolidoro has worked as a residential plot planner, where her drawings of other people's properties can be found in City Halls up and down the East coast, for a Concrete Company where she often scaled upwards of 10 feet to remove metal forms from the finished walls, as a secretary, a sandwich maker, a bartender, a tutor, a video editor, and a yoga instructor. She received her BS from Salem State University in 2011, where she finally found her writing 'tribe' and became a member of The Salem Writers Group.

She's an unofficial expert on Russian Literature, a poet and the founder of The Cellar, a monthly Spoken Word Open Mic that meets in Beverly, MA on the 2nd Thursday of every month. Her work has been published in a plethora of small journals that stretch from New England to San Francisco to England.

She currently lives in Woburn, MA with her youngest daughter, their two remaining cats, and a garden full of their many victims (the cats' victims that is).

Acknowledgements

Special thanks to Kevin Carey for being a kind and constructively critical teacher/mentor, for inviting me into the obscenely talented North Shore writing community, and for being the first person to encourage, guide, and champion my interest in writing and sharing my poetry.

Thanks also to these journals, who first published work from this collection:

Nude Bruce Review, "The Imp of the Perverse", July 2018, Issue 8

Incessant Pipe, "Eat the Damn Pie", April 2018

Soundings East, "Intervent", Spring 2018, Volume 40

Clockwise Cat, "The Inheritor", Spring/Summer 2015, Issue 31